HAL LEONARD *EVEN MORE* EASY POP MELODIES

GUITAR METHOD

Supplement to Any Guitar Method

THIRD EDITION

T0033953

INTRODUCTION

Welcome to *Even More Easy Pop Melodies*, a collection of 20 pop and rock favorites arranged for easy guitar. If you're a beginning guitarist, you've come to the right place; these well-known songs will have you playing, reading, and enjoying music in no time!

This collection can be used on its own or as a supplement to the *Hal Leonard Guitar Method* or any other beginning guitar method. The songs are arranged in order of difficulty. Each melody is presented in an easy-to-read format – including lyrics to help you follow along and chords for optional accompaniment (by your teacher, if you have one).

ISBN 978-0-7935-3235-3

HAL•LEONARD®

7777 W. BLUEMOUND RD. P.O. BOX 13819 MILWAUKEE, WI 53213

Visit Hal Leonard Online at
www.halleonard.com

SONG STRUCTURE

The songs in this book have different sections, which may or may not include the following:

Intro
This is usually a short instrumental section that "introduces" the song at the beginning.

Verse
This is one of the main sections of a song and conveys most of the storyline. A song usually has several verses, all with the same music but each with different lyrics.

Chorus
This is often the most memorable section of a song. Unlike the verse, the chorus usually has the same lyrics every time it repeats.

Bridge
This section is a break from the rest of the song, often having a very different chord progression and feel.

Solo
This is an instrumental section, often played over the verse or chorus structure.

Outro
Similar to an intro, this section brings the song to an end.

ENDINGS & REPEATS

Many of the songs have some new symbols that you must understand before playing. Each of these represents a different type of ending.

1st and 2nd Endings
These are indicated by brackets and numbers. The first time through a song section, play the first ending and then repeat. The second time through, skip the first ending, and play through the second ending.

D.S.
This means "Dal Segno" or "from the sign." When you see this abbreviation above the staff, find the sign (𝄋) earlier in the song and resume playing from that point.

al Coda
This means "to the Coda," a concluding section in the song. If you see the words "D.S. al Coda," return to the sign (𝄋) earlier in the song and play until you see the words "To Coda," then skip to the Coda at the end of the song, indicated by the symbol: ⊕.

al Fine
This means "to the end." If you see the words "D.S. al Fine," return to the sign (𝄋) earlier in the song and play until you see the word "Fine."

D.C.
This means "Da Capo" or "from the head." When you see this abbreviation above the staff, return to the beginning (or "head") of the song and resume playing.

CONTENTS

ELEANOR RIGBY

Words and Music by
John Lennon and Paul McCartney

CAN'T BUY ME LOVE

Words and Music by
John Lennon and Paul McCartney

HOME

Words and Music by
Greg Holden and Drew Pearson

home.

Verse

2. Set-tle down, _____ it-'ll all be

clear.

Don't pay no mind to the de-mons; they fill you with

tear.

Trou-ble, it might drag you down. You get

lost, you can al-ways be found. Just know you're not a-lone, _____

'cause I'm gon-na make this place your home.

Outro

Repeat and fade

Oo, _____ oo. _____

9

ANOTHER BRICK IN THE WALL

Words and Music by
Roger Waters

Verse

1., 2. We don't need __ no ed - u - ca - tion.

We don't need __ no thought con - trol, __

no dark sar - cas __ m

in the class - room.

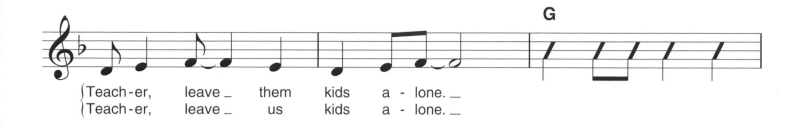

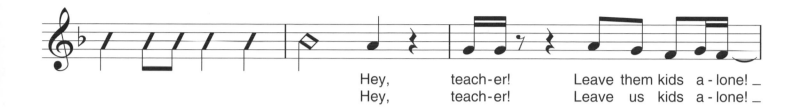
(Teach-er, leave _ them kids a - lone. _
(Teach-er, leave _ us kids a - lone. _

Hey, teach-er! Leave them kids a - lone! _
Hey, teach-er! Leave us kids a - lone! _

Chorus

_ All in all, _ it's just an -
_ All in all, _ you're just an -

- oth - er brick in the wall.)
- oth - er brick in the wall.)

All in all, _ you're just an - oth - er brick in the

Dm
wall.

HEY, SOUL SISTER

Words and Music by Pat Monahan,
Espen Lind and Amund Bjorklund

STAY WITH ME

Words and Music by Sam Smith,
James Napier, William Edward Phillips,
Tom Petty and Jeff Lynne

1. Guess it's true, I'm not good at a one-night stand.
2. Why am I so e-mo-tion-al?

But I still need love 'cause I'm just a man.
No, it's not a good look. Gain some self-con-trol.

These nights nev-er seem to go to plan.
And deep down I ___ know this nev-er works.

I don't want you to leave, will you hold my hand?
But you can lay with me so it does-n't hurt.

Oh, won't you

Chorus

stay _____ with me? _____ 'Cause you're all _____ I need. _____

_____ This ain't _____ love, it's clear to see. _____ But dar-ling,

3rd time, to Coda

1. stay _____ with me. _____

2. Oh, _____

Bridge

_____ oh, _____ oh. _

1. _____ Oh, _____ _____

2. *D.S. al Coda* Oh, won't you

Coda

_____

15

(SITTIN' ON) THE DOCK OF THE BAY

Words and Music by
Steve Cropper and Otis Redding

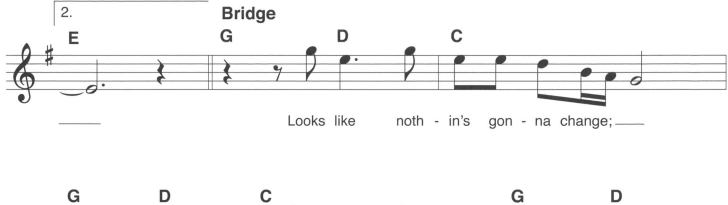

Bridge

Looks like noth - in's gon - na change; _____

ev - 'ry - thing still _____ re - mains the _____ same. _____ I can't do what

ten peo - ple tell me to do, so I guess I'll re - main _____ the same.

Coda   **Outro**

Repeat and fade

ANOTHER ONE BITES THE DUST

Words and Music by
John Deacon

An - oth - er one bites the dust. ___ And an -

oth - er one gone, and an - oth - er one gone, an - oth - er one bites the dust. ___

Hey! ___ I'm gon - na get you, too, an - oth - er one bites the dust. ___

Outro

Repeat and fade

CRAZY TRAIN

Words and Music by
Ozzy Osbourne, Randy Rhoads
and Bob Daisley

1. Cra - zy, but that's how it goes. _____
(2.) lis - tened to preach - ers, I've lis - tened to fools. _____ I've

Mil-lions of peo - ple liv - ing as foes. _____
watched all the drop - outs who make their own rules. _____

May - be _____ it's not too late _____
One per - son con - di - tioned to rule and control. ____

_____ to learn how to love, ____
_____ The me - di - a sells it,

and for - get how to hate. _____
and you live the role. _____

Chorus

Men - tal wounds ___ not heal - ing, life's a bit - ter shame. ___
Men - tal wounds ___ still scream - ing, driv - ing me ___ in - sane. ___

I'm go - ing off ___ the rails ___ on a cra - zy train. ___

_____ I'm go - ing off ___ the rails ___

on a cra-zy train.

2. I've

Bridge

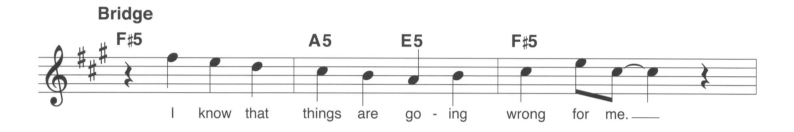

I know that things are go - ing wrong for me.

You've got - ta lis - ten — to my

Guitar Solo

words, — yeah, — yeah! —

Fade out

—

HEART SHAPED BOX

Words and Music by
Kurt Cobain

Drop D tuning:
(low to high) D-A-D-G-B-E

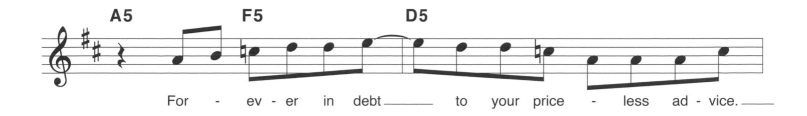

For - ev - er in debt _____ to your price - less ad - vice. _____

_____ Hey! Wait! I've got a new com - plaint.

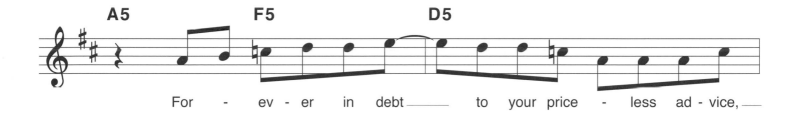

For - ev - er in debt _____ to your price - less ad - vice, _____

_____ your ad - vice. _____

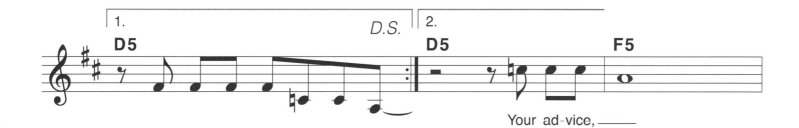

Your ad - vice, _____

your ad-vice. _____

Runaway

Words and Music by
Max Crook and Del Shannon

wo - wo - wo - wo - won - der. ___

Why, ___ why, why, why, why, why, she ran a - way, ___

___ and ___ I won - der where she will stay, ___

___ my lit - tle run - a - way, ___ a

run - run - run - run - run - a - way. ___

run - a - way, ___ a run - run - run - run -

TEQUILA

By Chuck Rio

Intro

(spoken:) Tequila!

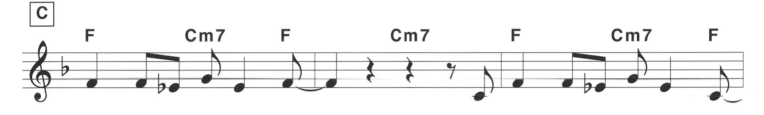

(spoken:) Tequila!

YESTERDAY

Words and Music by
John Lennon and Paul McCartney

GOOD VIBRATIONS

Words and Music by
Brian Wilson and Mike Love

33

21 GUNS

Words and Music by David Bowie,
John Phillips, Billie Joe and Green Day

Additional Lyrics

3. When it's time to live and let die
   And you can't get another try,
   Something inside this heart has died.
   You're in ruins.

ROLLING IN THE DEEP

Words and Music by
Adele Adkins and Paul Epworth

think-ing that we al-most had it all. The scars of your ___ love, they leave me

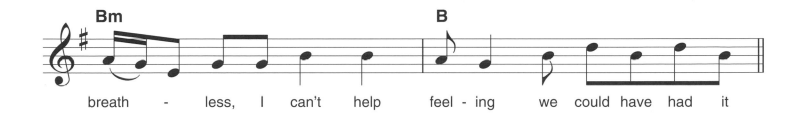

breath - less, I can't help feel - ing we could have had it

Chorus

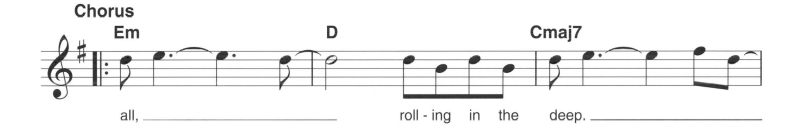

all, _____ roll - ing in the deep. _____

___ You had my heart in - side _____ of your hand, _____ {and / but} you played _

___ it _____ to the beat. _____ We could have had it

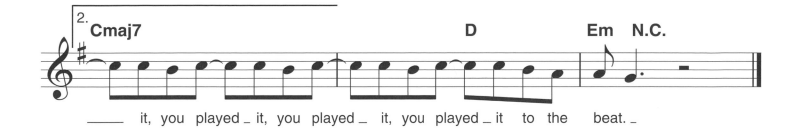

_____ it, you played _ it, you played _ it, you played _ it to the beat. _

HALLELUJAH

Words and Music by
Leonard Cohen

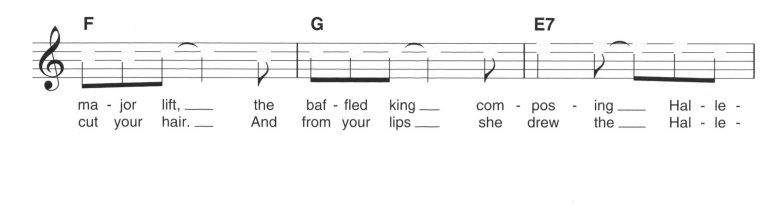

ma - jor lift, ___ the baf - fled king ___ com - pos - ing ___ Hal - le -
cut your hair. ___ And from your lips ___ she drew the ___ Hal - le -

𝄋 Chorus

lu - jah. ___
lu - jah. ___ Hal - le - lu - jah, ___ Ha - le -

lu - jah, ___ Hal - le - lu - jah, ___ Hal - le -

3rd time, to Coda 🜚

lu jah. 2. Your

D.S. al Coda

jah. Hal - le -

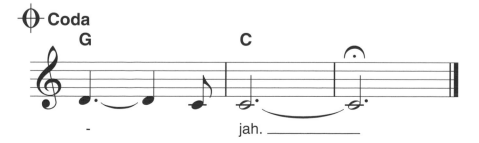

🜚 **Coda**

- jah. ___

Sleepwalk

By Santo Farina,
John Farina and Ann Farina

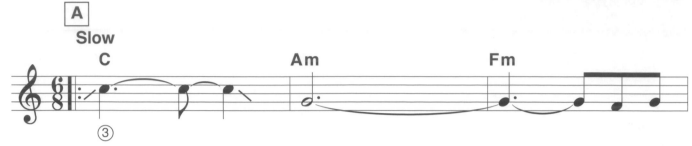

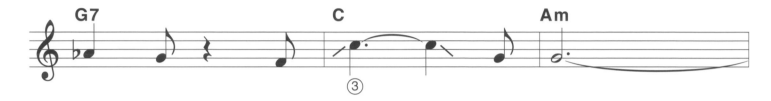

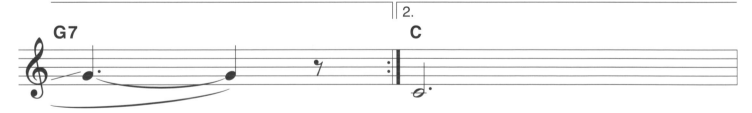

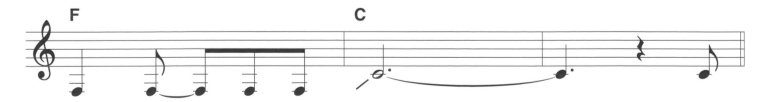

D.C. al Coda

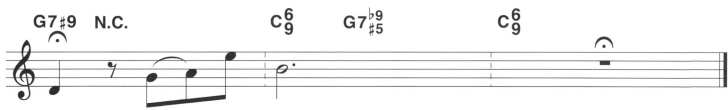

SEA OF LOVE

Words and Music by
George Khoury and Philip Baptiste

Verse

1., 3. Do you re - mem - ber ___ when ___ we met? ___
2. Come ___ with me, ___ my ___ love, ___

That's the day ___ I knew you were my pet.
to the sea, ___ the sea ___ of ___ love.

I ___ want to tell you how ___ much I

love you. ___

Chorus

Come ___ with me ___ to ___ the sea ___

___ of love. ___

Coda

love you. _____

Chorus

Come _____ with me to _____ the sea _____

_____ of love. _____

Verse

4. Come with me, _____ my _____ love, _____ to the sea, _____ the

sea _____ of love. _____ I _____ want to tell you just _____ how much I

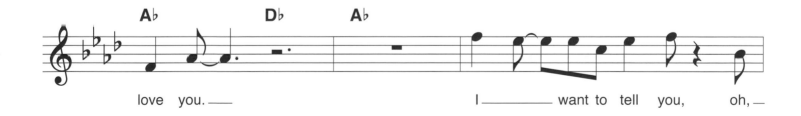

love you. _____ I _____ want to tell you, oh, _____

_____ how _____ much _____ I love you. _____

rit.

CRAZY

Words and Music by
Willie Nelson

won - d'rin' _____ what in the world did I do? _____

Chorus

_____ Cra - zy _____ for think - ing that my love could

hold you; _____ I'm cra - zy for try - in', _____

cra - zy for cry - in', _____ and I'm cra - zy for lov - in'

Chorus

you. Cra - zy _____ for think - ing that my love could

hold you; _____ I'm cra - zy for try - in', _____

cra - zy for cry - in', _____ and I'm cra - zy for lov - in' you.

rit.

HAL LEONARD GUITAR METHOD

METHOD BOOKS, SONGBOOKS AND REFERENCE BOOKS

THE HAL LEONARD GUITAR METHOD is designed for anyone just learning to play acoustic or electric guitar. It is based on years of teaching guitar students of all ages, and it also reflects some of the best guitar teaching ideas from around the world. This comprehensive method includes: A learning sequence carefully paced with clear instructions; popular songs which increase the incentive to learn to play; versatility – can be used as self-instruction or with a teacher; audio accompaniments so that students have fun and sound great while practicing.

BOOK 1
00699010	Book Only	$8.99
00699027	Book/Online Audio	$12.99
00697341	Book/Online Audio + DVD	$24.99
00697318	DVD Only	$19.99
00155480	Deluxe Beginner Edition (Book, CD, DVD, Online Audio/ Video & Chord Poster)	$19.99

COMPLETE (BOOKS 1, 2 & 3)
00699040	Book Only	$16.99
00697342	Book/Online Audio	$24.99

BOOK 2
00699020	Book Only	$8.99
00697313	Book/Online Audio	$12.99

BOOK 3
00699030	Book Only	$8.99
00697316	Book/Online Audio	$12.99

Prices, contents and availability subject to change without notice.

STYLISTIC METHODS

ACOUSTIC GUITAR
00697347	Method Book/Online Audio	$17.99
00237969	Songbook/Online Audio	$16.99

BLUEGRASS GUITAR
00697405	Method Book/Online Audio	$16.99

BLUES GUITAR
00697326	Method Book/Online Audio (9" x 12")	$16.99
00697344	Method Book/Online Audio (6" x 9")	$15.99
00697385	Songbook/Online Audio (9" x 12")	$14.99
00248636	Kids Method Book/Online Audio	$12.99

BRAZILIAN GUITAR
00697415	Method Book/Online Audio	$17.99

CHRISTIAN GUITAR
00695947	Method Book/Online Audio	$16.99
00697408	Songbook/CD Pack	$14.99

CLASSICAL GUITAR
00697376	Method Book/Online Audio	$15.99

COUNTRY GUITAR
00697337	Method Book/Online Audio	$22.99
00697400	Songbook/Online Audio	$19.99

FINGERSTYLE GUITAR
00697378	Method Book/Online Audio	$21.99
00697432	Songbook/Online Audio	$16.99

FLAMENCO GUITAR
00697363	Method Book/Online Audio	$15.99

FOLK GUITAR
00697414	Method Book/Online Audio	$16.99

JAZZ GUITAR
00695359	Book/Online Audio	$22.99
00697386	Songbook/Online Audio	$15.99

JAZZ-ROCK FUSION
00697387	Book/Online Audio	$24.99

R&B GUITAR
00697356	Book/Online Audio	$19.99
00697433	Songbook/CD Pack	$14.99

ROCK GUITAR
00697319	Book/Online Audio	$16.99
00697383	Songbook/Online Audio	$16.99

ROCKABILLY GUITAR
00697407	Book/Online Audio	$16.99

OTHER METHOD BOOKS

BARITONE GUITAR METHOD
00242055	Book/Online Audio	$12.99

GUITAR FOR KIDS
00865003	Method Book 1/Online Audio	$12.99
00697402	Songbook/Online Audio	$9.99
00128437	Method Book 2/Online Audio	$12.99

MUSIC THEORY FOR GUITARISTS
00695790	Book/Online Audio	$19.99

TENOR GUITAR METHOD
00148330	Book/Online Audio	$12.99

12-STRING GUITAR METHOD
00249528	Book/Online Audio	$19.99

METHOD SUPPLEMENTS

ARPEGGIO FINDER
00697352	6" x 9" Edition	$6.99
00697351	9" x 12" Edition	$9.99

BARRE CHORDS
00697406	Book/Online Audio	$14.99

CHORD, SCALE & ARPEGGIO FINDER
00697410	Book Only	$19.99

GUITAR TECHNIQUES
00697389	Book/Online Audio	$16.99

INCREDIBLE CHORD FINDER
00697200	6" x 9" Edition	$7.99
00697208	9" x 12" Edition	$7.99

INCREDIBLE SCALE FINDER
00695568	6" x 9" Edition	$9.99
00695490	9" x 12" Edition	$9.99

LEAD LICKS
00697345	Book/Online Audio	$10.99

RHYTHM RIFFS
00697346	Book/Online Audio	$14.99

SONGBOOKS

CLASSICAL GUITAR PIECES
00697388	Book/Online Audio	$9.99

EASY POP MELODIES
00697281	Book Only	$7.99
00697440	Book/Online Audio	$14.99

(MORE) EASY POP MELODIES
00697280	Book Only	$6.99
00697269	Book/Online Audio	$14.99

(EVEN MORE) EASY POP MELODIES
00699154	Book Only	$6.99
00697439	Book/Online Audio	$14.99

EASY POP RHYTHMS
00697336	Book Only	$7.99
00697441	Book/Online Audio	$14.99

(MORE) EASY POP RHYTHMS
00697338	Book Only	$7.99
00697322	Book/Online Audio	$14.99

(EVEN MORE) EASY POP RHYTHMS
00697340	Book Only	$7.99
00697323	Book/Online Audio	$14.99

EASY POP CHRISTMAS MELODIES
00697417	Book Only	$9.99
00697416	Book/Online Audio	$14.99

EASY POP CHRISTMAS RHYTHMS
00278177	Book Only	$6.99
00278175	Book/Online Audio	$14.99

EASY SOLO GUITAR PIECES
00110407	Book Only	$9.99

REFERENCE

GUITAR PRACTICE PLANNER
00697401	Book Only	$5.99

GUITAR SETUP & MAINTENANCE
00697427	6" x 9" Edition	$14.99
00697421	9" x 12" Edition	$12.99

For more info, songlists, or to purchase these and more books from your favorite music retailer, go to

halleonard.com

HAL•LEONARD®

EASY GUITAR WITH NOTES & TAB

This series features simplified arrangements with notes, tab, chord charts, and strum and pick patterns.

MIXED FOLIOS

00702287	Acoustic	$19.99
00702002	Acoustic Rock Hits for Easy Guitar	$15.99
00702166	All-Time Best Guitar Collection	$19.99
00702232	Best Acoustic Songs for Easy Guitar	$16.99
00119835	Best Children's Songs	$16.99
00703055	The Big Book of Nursery Rhymes & Children's Songs	$16.99
00698978	Big Christmas Collection	$19.99
00702394	Bluegrass Songs for Easy Guitar	$15.99
00289632	Bohemian Rhapsody	$19.99
00703387	Celtic Classics	$14.99
00224808	Chart Hits of 2016-2017	$14.99
00267383	Chart Hits of 2017-2018	$14.99
00334293	Chart Hits of 2019-2020	$16.99
00702149	Children's Christian Songbook	$9.99
00702028	Christmas Classics	$8.99
00101779	Christmas Guitar	$14.99
00702141	Classic Rock	$8.95
00159642	Classical Melodies	$12.99
00253933	Disney/Pixar's Coco	$16.99
00702203	CMT's 100 Greatest Country Songs	$34.99
00702283	The Contemporary Christian Collection	$16.99
00196954	Contemporary Disney	$19.99
00702239	Country Classics for Easy Guitar	$24.99

00702257	Easy Acoustic Guitar Songs	$16.99
00702041	Favorite Hymns for Easy Guitar	$12.99
00222701	Folk Pop Songs	$17.99
00126894	Frozen	$14.99
00333922	Frozen 2	$14.99
00702286	Glee	$16.99
00702160	The Great American Country Songbook	$19.99
00702148	Great American Gospel for Guitar	$14.99
00702050	Great Classical Themes for Easy Guitar	$9.99
00275088	The Greatest Showman	$17.99
00148030	Halloween Guitar Songs	$14.99
00702273	Irish Songs	$12.99
00192503	Jazz Classics for Easy Guitar	$16.99
00702275	Jazz Favorites for Easy Guitar	$17.99
00702274	Jazz Standards for Easy Guitar	$19.99
00702162	Jumbo Easy Guitar Songbook	$24.99
00232285	La La Land	$16.99
00702258	Legends of Rock	$14.99
00702189	MTV's 100 Greatest Pop Songs	$34.99
00702272	1950s Rock	$16.99
00702271	1960s Rock	$16.99
00702270	1970s Rock	$19.99
00702269	1980s Rock	$15.99
00702268	1990s Rock	$19.99
00369043	Rock Songs for Kids	$14.99

00109725	Once	$14.99
00702187	Selections from O Brother Where Art Thou?	$19.99
00702178	100 Songs for Kids	$14.99
00702515	Pirates of the Caribbean	$17.99
00702125	Praise and Worship for Guitar	$14.99
00287930	Songs from A Star Is Born, The Greatest Showman, La La Land, and More Movie Musicals	$16.99
00702285	Southern Rock Hits	$12.99
00156420	Star Wars Music	$16.99
00121535	30 Easy Celtic Guitar Solos	$16.99
00702156	3-Chord Rock	$12.99
00244654	Top Hits of 2017	$14.99
00283786	Top Hits of 2018	$14.99
00702294	Top Worship Hits	$17.99
00702255	VH1's 100 Greatest Hard Rock Songs	$34.99
00702175	VH1's 100 Greatest Songs of Rock and Roll	$29.99
00702253	Wicked	$12.99

ARTIST COLLECTIONS

00702267	AC/DC for Easy Guitar	$16.99
00702598	Adele for Easy Guitar	$15.99
00156221	Adele – 25	$16.99
00702040	Best of the Allman Brothers	$16.99
00702865	J.S. Bach for Easy Guitar	$15.99
00702169	Best of The Beach Boys	$15.99
00702292	The Beatles — 1	$22.99
00125796	Best of Chuck Berry	$15.99
00702201	The Essential Black Sabbath	$15.99
00702250	blink-182 — Greatest Hits	$17.99
02501615	Zac Brown Band — The Foundation	$17.99
02501621	Zac Brown Band — You Get What You Give	$16.99
00702043	Best of Johnny Cash	$17.99
00702090	Eric Clapton's Best	$16.99
00702086	Eric Clapton — from the Album Unplugged	$17.99
00702202	The Essential Eric Clapton	$17.99
00702053	Best of Patsy Cline	$15.99
00222697	Very Best of Coldplay – 2nd Edition	$16.99
00702229	The Very Best of Creedence Clearwater Revival	$16.99
00702145	Best of Jim Croce	$16.99
00702278	Crosby, Stills & Nash	$12.99
14042809	Bob Dylan	$15.99
00702276	Fleetwood Mac — Easy Guitar Collection	$17.99
00139462	The Very Best of Grateful Dead	$16.99
00702136	Best of Merle Haggard	$16.99
00702227	Jimi Hendrix — Smash Hits	$19.99
00702288	Best of Hillsong United	$12.99
00702236	Best of Antonio Carlos Jobim	$15.99
00702245	Elton John — Greatest Hits 1970–2002	$19.99

00129855	Jack Johnson	$16.99
00702204	Robert Johnson	$14.99
00702234	Selections from Toby Keith — 35 Biggest Hits	$12.95
00702003	Kiss	$16.99
00702216	Lynyrd Skynyrd	$16.99
00702182	The Essential Bob Marley	$16.99
00146081	Maroon 5	$14.99
00121925	Bruno Mars — Unorthodox Jukebox	$12.99
00702248	Paul McCartney — All the Best	$14.99
00125484	The Best of MercyMe	$12.99
00702209	Steve Miller Band — Young Hearts (Greatest Hits)	$12.95
00124167	Jason Mraz	$15.99
00702096	Best of Nirvana	$16.99
00702211	The Offspring — Greatest Hits	$17.99
00138026	One Direction	$17.99
00702030	Best of Roy Orbison	$17.99
00702144	Best of Ozzy Osbourne	$14.99
00702279	Tom Petty	$17.99
00102911	Pink Floyd	$17.99
00702139	Elvis Country Favorites	$19.99
00702293	The Very Best of Prince	$19.99
00699415	Best of Queen for Guitar	$16.99
00109279	Best of R.E.M.	$14.99
00702208	Red Hot Chili Peppers — Greatest Hits	$16.99
00198960	The Rolling Stones	$17.99
00174793	The Very Best of Santana	$16.99
00702196	Best of Bob Seger	$16.99
00146046	Ed Sheeran	$15.99
00702252	Frank Sinatra — Nothing But the Best	$12.99
00702010	Best of Rod Stewart	$17.99
00702049	Best of George Strait	$17.99

00702259	Taylor Swift for Easy Guitar	$15.99
00359800	Taylor Swift – Easy Guitar Anthology	$24.99
00702260	Taylor Swift — Fearless	$14.99
00139727	Taylor Swift — 1989	$17.99
00115960	Taylor Swift — Red	$16.99
00253667	Taylor Swift — Reputation	$17.99
00702290	Taylor Swift — Speak Now	$16.99
00232849	Chris Tomlin Collection – 2nd Edition	$14.99
00702226	Chris Tomlin — See the Morning	$12.95
00148643	Train	$14.99
00702427	U2 — 18 Singles	$19.99
00702108	Best of Stevie Ray Vaughan	$17.99
00279005	The Who	$14.99
00702123	Best of Hank Williams	$15.99
00194548	Best of John Williams	$14.99
00702228	Neil Young — Greatest Hits	$17.99
00119133	Neil Young — Harvest	$14.99

HAL•LEONARD®

Visit Hal Leonard online at **halleonard.com**

Guitar Chord Songbooks

Each 6" x 9" book includes complete lyrics, chord symbols, and guitar chord diagrams.

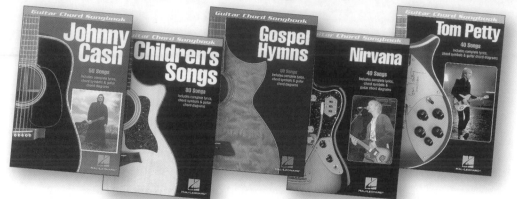

Acoustic Hits
00701787 . . . . $14.99

Acoustic Rock
00699540 . . . . $22.99

Alabama
00699914 . . . . $14.95

The Beach Boys
00699566 . . . . $19.99

Bluegrass
00702585 . . . . $14.99

Johnny Cash
00699648 . . . . $19.99

Children's Songs
00699539 . . . . $17.99

Christmas Carols
00699536 . . . . $14.99

Christmas Songs
00119911 . . . . $14.99

Eric Clapton
00699567 . . . . $19.99

Classic Rock
00699598 . . . . $20.99

Coffeehouse Hits
00703318 . . . . $14.99

Country
00699534 . . . . $17.99

Country Favorites
00700609 . . . . $14.99

Country Hits
00140859 . . . . $14.99

Country Standards
00700608 . . . . $12.95

Cowboy Songs
00699636 . . . . $19.99

Creedence Clearwater Revival
00701786 . . . . $16.99

Jim Croce
00148087 . . . . $14.99

Crosby, Stills & Nash
00701609 . . . . $16.99

John Denver
02501697 . . . . $17.99

Neil Diamond
00700606 . . . . $19.99

Disney – 2nd Edition
00295786 . . . . $17.99

The Doors
00699888 . . . . $19.99

Eagles
00122917 . . . . $17.99

Early Rock
00699916 . . . . $14.99

Folksongs
00699541 . . . . $14.99

Folk Pop Rock
00699651 . . . . $17.99

40 Easy Strumming Songs
00115972 . . . . $16.99

Four Chord Songs
00701611 . . . . $15.99

Glee
00702501 . . . . $14.99

Gospel Hymns
00700463 . . . . $16.99

Grand Ole Opry®
00699885 . . . . $16.95

Grateful Dead
00139461 . . . . $16.99

Green Day
00103074 . . . . $16.99

Irish Songs
00701044 . . . . $16.99

Michael Jackson
00137847 . . . . $14.99

Billy Joel
00699632 . . . . $19.99

Elton John
00699732 . . . . $17.99

Ray LaMontagne
00130337 . . . . $12.99

Latin Songs
00700973 . . . . $14.99

Love Songs
00701043 . . . . $14.99

Bob Marley
00701704 . . . . $17.99

Bruno Mars
00125332 . . . . $12.99

Paul McCartney
00385035 . . . . $16.95

Steve Miller
00701146 . . . . $12.99

Modern Worship
00701801 . . . . $16.99

Motown
00699734 . . . . $19.99

Willie Nelson
00148273 . . . . $17.99

Nirvana
00699762 . . . . $17.99

Roy Orbison
00699752 . . . . $19.99

Peter, Paul & Mary
00103013 . . . . $19.99

Tom Petty
00699883 . . . . $17.99

Pink Floyd
00139116 . . . . $17.99

Pop/Rock
00699538 . . . . $16.99

Praise & Worship
00699634 . . . . $14.99

Elvis Presley
00699633 . . . . $17.99

Queen
00702395 . . . . $14.99

Red Hot Chili Peppers
00699710 . . . . $24.99

The Rolling Stones
00137716 . . . . $19.99

Bob Seger
00701147 . . . . $12.99

Carly Simon
00121011 . . . . $14.99

Sting
00699921 . . . . $24.99

Three Chord Acoustic Songs
00123860 . . . . $14.99

Three Chord Songs
00699720 . . . . $17.99

Two-Chord Songs
00119236 . . . . $16.99

U2
00137744 . . . . $19.99

Hank Williams
00700607 . . . . $16.99

Stevie Wonder
00120862 . . . . $14.99

Prices and availability subject to change without notice.

Visit Hal Leonard online at **www.halleonard.com**